(AT) WRIST

(AT) WRIST

Tacey M. Atsitty

THE UNIVERSITY OF WISCONSIN PRESS

Publication of this book has been made possible, in part, through support from the Brittingham Trust.

The University of Wisconsin Press
728 State Street, Suite 443
Madison, Wisconsin 53706
uwpress.wisc.edu

Gray's Inn House, 127 Clerkenwell Road
London EC1R 5DB, United Kingdom
eurospanbookstore.com

Printed in the United States of America
This book may be available in a digital edition.

Library of Congress Cataloging-in-Publication Data
Names: Atsitty, Tacey M., 1982- author.
Title: (At) wrist / Tacey M. Atsitty.
Other titles: Wisconsin poetry series.
Description: Madison, Wisconsin : The University of Wisconsin Press, 2023. |
Series: Wisconsin poetry series
Identifiers: LCCN 2023015310 | ISBN 9780299346546 (paperback)
Subjects: LCGFT: Poetry.
Classification: LCC PS3601.T75 A9 2023 | DDC 811/.6—dc23/eng/20230628
LC record available at https://lccn.loc.gov/2023015310

To shizhé'é
and
every man who extended me his wrist

Life will break you. Nobody can protect you from that, and living alone won't either, for solitude will also break you with its yearning. You have to love. You have to feel. It is the reason you are here on earth. You are here to risk your heart. You are here to be swallowed up. And when it happens that you are broken, or betrayed, or left, or hurt, or death brushes near, let yourself sit by an apple tree and listen to the apples falling all around you in heaps, wasting their sweetness. Tell yourself that you tasted as many as you could.

—LOUISE ERDRICH

Contents

) (

( )

A February Snow

I thought I knew love in every drag
of the tongue across icing, sparkle

in glaze, thought I went wading
into stars, pulling my dress up

to my knees—I get like this
when it precipitates: fall

like salt. Muscles in my back tear
to the point of floating, bearing

flakes. They come heavy now,
lacking grace, exposing the weight

my collarbones carry. The wind
can only lift so much with its song:

snow is a blessing; its color
amplifies silence, so you can hear

every crunch or offering of self:
a sugar cookie wrapped in napkin.

Alas, all that's here is a field
of snow & a napkin to cleanse

my lips of any leftover sweetness.
I ate that cookie for days, until I fell

brittle. It's the time of year when I sink
into my armchair, into threads

of branches gone bare. It's tough to tell
in this scene if it's birth or dying

time. All I know is it's the season
when wind comes crying, like a baby

whose head knocks a pew during the passing
of the sacrament, that silence—

her long inhale filling with pain.

Sonnet for My Wrist

I tend to mistake your ribs for a hand towel,
it hangs on a nail above the washbowl, the hand towel,
ripped. There's something wearing about the end curve
of thread. When I sleep I keep my palms open. Verve:
We were lovers in a field of gray. In Navajo, we say something
rote: I'll radical when you hurt me something
close, even you waft—it's best I tether, forget flyaways
I plucked. My bones, they lay, to me, like fray. Like gaunt:
I don't crawl back for fragments, even a spinal cord
of sinew—it's not going to close. You rope
me from stray to grip: it's all for naught. I'm born
for my father, Tangle People. Our mouths in webs:
tonight my wrists part, and you chase my insides
until they dangle into pieces.

Bird Dance

The nice thing about tree rings
is tomorrow they'll curve

out of themselves, stay beneath
blossom, or shoot off

into each other; they'll grow
then gray into each other—

to delineate one from another
is like pulling at centipede grass:

you'll pull up the entire lawn
or forest, leaving only skinfolds

of earthen mounds, carved out
wrist story of Monster Slayer:

in a virgin creek, leg & thigh
of his mother soak

up the Sun. Immaculate
pulse of radiance & ripple

in her soon rounded
middle, jut out for (f)all—

longer than any concentric
season, dark and dry

circles reveal a tree split
open, what is found between

arm bones—a kind of sheet
music with all whole notes,

this is how rings sing
in the early morn, a choral

of cicadas sound *come, come*
as though they had wrists

to shake gourds at His coming.

Round Our Wrists
for First Man

We swing like shawls about the shoulders of brides,
spread open in a field of snow. Though it's just yet fall,
leaves bob red, foretell the absence of voice at eventide.

Once we sat in the current of a longhouse, lolled
in memory of a stew that warmed an ice monster. I raked
the story for your elbow and warmth: a message so petty.

I missed you when you left to carve a snow-snake
tunnel. Upon throwing, my tendon caught in the eddy
of creation. I could no longer lift logs to stack,

this was love in the saying: I could only follow your collar
in snow so far. (Bark I braided round our wrists round back).
One of these days you will find me under the white—

where autumn floats, rounding out the soles
of our feet, where the arcs of our breaths hold.

Out of Star

Float in to apologize, the first and easiest—our hands
To purge the pulse I felt right here, on my tongue

In the buds of each petal, the pillowcase I hand-stitched
He said he'd use it to pass through clouds on his way

One morning, he buoyed me with his tide and rock
Like something out of a summer blow along the shores

Or a boy that winds through Russian olives at sunset
I've floated that river over and over and back into child

The morning I drove from the sun, then walked into it
How could he not feel this whir for him, when I lifted his couch

Inside out, and even when I uttered every mourning, at every rill
For every watercourse that never turned out, in voice nor text

Why, in the final sunrise of our breaths, could he not see the still
As gold riffed from my eyes into his

Sang Over

pile like leaves   or rake
into sunset   past over   ever fallen
look   into gold   & every pyramid
left   loose   into circles   this argument
dive   and no more   debris for   ever
autumn branches   of the once evergreen
lie in corners, where   winter left   them
reasoning like that, having gone maculate before
they were swept   over   then sang over
since on the radio, in truck, abandon
mimic of   leaf shed since   leave   lyrics
to anyone   else's veins to be   so blatantly—
no longer fall into   logic with   neck or organ
or heave over what's left   the apricot stump
so now dusk   shines through blinds   and finally—
flaw—over   leaves rake into circles

Chafe

For someone husky, like me, it's grained
at the inner thighs. Like rubbing a corn tassel,
between your thumb and fingers until it looses.
Or even just bumping it with a thick stick, losing

pollen when it's time. I know how stalks loosen:
I've seen Dad tie them when they'd lean too far,
almost to the ground. Their brace roots exposed
from wind or too much water, gentle rustles

in wind or breath, deep bends at the knees.
Once depending alone on rain, once sprouting
silken, firm—closer we are to being round—
until the turns of girdling. Until the drop to humus,
no longer embarrassed at such a thin weave:
legs—skin—leaf—limb—

Apricot Lament

Just when he thought to loom the backyard for bud &
Just when he came to admire, or thought to dote over
Already he rues stick-thin arms, whose petals brave the late
Whose middles freeze; we've gone without
All ramose till now, empty skirts anxious to round back for
It's the fourth year lips have gone without any such
Already hips full of leaves and none
Else, years by last, the lone—it splat behind
My back, it came to ache as the rake clawed
We've gone into partial burn, without even
No matter for bloom, the seasons no longer allow
The trouble with doting over blossoms is
In a swollen tub of ruth, wanting nothing but his

Hole through the Rock

I was something slough before you rode me silver. And smooth,
until shone. I rode in and didn't even see I was gone: the eye

of my navel, sand folds this way all the time. And rain scours
just the same. You hold all the clay. I fall to granule.

But within my whorl, you are winged: doubled and pure,
like the coupling of pebbles in storm water. These enduring

glances from wind on pane say you can see plainly the part
of me you miss. Our palms meet at the fingertips, forming a *W*:

double, which is only half me to whole us. Where our wrists
brush smooth, clay chips curve into this sand-swept hollow:

a roil to the usual clink of bone and arc in stone.

Querido Apu
Cali, Colombia

I carry a meter of fabric from your mother's store
to wrap myself in: in can, in gourd. Apu, you are

abalone. I turn to your hand on my spine, a calm
parting of words. Así es, Apu. Strings of shells

above your head, shift with our bodies;
tonight I come unbraided, as fragile as wind

curling about the bars of your windows. I bury
myself in yards of recitation like the women

chanting inside. This is all I remember:
Could I be the wife of a trinket seller

at the feet of three crosses and a bulbed
Christ, renouncing letter & skin. Could I for beauty

of round eyes & shared skin—In my lap rests a box
filled with bent hearts & black night angles. Outside,

a boy bends charms: silver-wired flower, sun and sperm.
Stories hand-shaped and given to carry, to keep. A wish

of fertility in my pocket. Could I sing the shadows
of untangling, for your mother for Christ for beauty

from the edges that ebb us in—Could I ascend water
rounding over and carry my voice above strands

at the second breaking to wade to wash. Could I adore
her, like your people once did—I'm sorry, Apu, I was

lost to the falls between us. And for all your calling,
I could only bear you here, where my pages curl.

Lace Sonnet

Like this vein:
webbed, glass
me a ribbon so rain,
so pearl in mass
or my wedding white
I see you at the crown
of my crux. Light
and petals veil, blown
this fringe. This leaf-
let face, let lips
drown the way. Your
coral neck, it zips
at the back: up
& down. My hand cup—

Still Life Morrow

Turn off the static, my therapist says.
Taste what you swallow. Inside, I feel

water burst from the baby bellas. I wish
I were staring at a still life, a bowl of cactus

fruit maybe, or rotted watermelon, and not
this wintry scene of the road I've just taken.

I think they know—about every leaf
I'd catch to peel from my tongue.

It spoke to how good I was at being
alone. This morning I sit in the still

kitchen, rued by autumn passing me by.
In it, rises our breath to the lone mountains,

as layers of rain gloss us abundantly.

River Silt

Water levels have bled out,
like it had just bitten its lip
& was about to swell—then rip:
had I paid better attention to drought,
listened more to the crows and stayed
with mountain clouds, I'd have let go
of the knot swing hanging above the slow
life flow beneath my legs, I'd have prayed

to forget all the times he came to me
but not wanted me: how fast it rises,
carrying plumes of pang in undercurrent:
swirls of sediment & silt around my knees—
the dragging stalks and leaves of irises,
how pathetic they look breaking in torrent—

The Night My Wrist Broke

The night snow fell so gently I mistook it
for female. They came ready for blood.

My dad raised me better than this—
five male EMTs peered into the light

of my truck. Their eyes scanned every dark
crease of my body—it was cold. That night

my truck was a cage protecting me, still—
I could hardly exhale: *I'm sorry I am crying.*

All but one looked away, allowing me to cry
for a moment longer, as though I were one

of them. I kept my right wrist close to my chest:
a pain so clear I could see every empty cavity

in my ribcage, heart thumping like a bass guitar—
hand strumming to the sound of a girl wailing.

Last Night, Bleeding

It had been years since I had bled this way,
and I had forgotten how to care for myself.

Last night when the prophet was near done
dying, I lay seeping into my new mattress.

Like Tom's dad, he gave them the slip,
the cells of his body—went in a calm yellow

way. Tom texted a photo of his father's head,
bald—the way my hands were going

from rubbing out blood from beneath
me and inside me, from my garments

and Christ, He welcomed his chosen seer
at the same time. Only yesterday did I see

the feet of a stillborn on Facebook. His toes
and soles and ankles already so pale

and peaceful in a cloud of sheets, while
the rest of us turn and turn in snow,

clotting back into white cells—then a code
talker, a grandfather, how handsome

his life and an American flag lies over—
these mornings I take to the rain

channel on YouTube, without thunder
so it feels real in season. These days,

every time I lie down I imagine cutting
the skin from my navel to my neck,

opening up like I've never done before

()

A Blood Letting

    it's taken me   to pulse down   entire solace

    of my truck, stars   night roads, hush   my own sister

       she shoots right   through

    me, I saw   from overpass

from mountains   arches & rocks   slats I've come to know

    every ridgeline, tilt   slit into earth   these years

    each formation   winds, cries

into mouth   a canyon, a set   of eyes glass over   from big wind

     —incise—   —fault line—   —

did you pass   me, I ask   oh,   she cuts, there's no time
    I   gauze   into my wrist, years or rivers
since our mother   has died, years or blue   since calm comes
    down again, think   how stars came to float

in bloodline: same   through our wrists   telling of the same

mother who left
us, who le t us—
and my sister le t

me, kneeling roadside   graveling, our veins   no longer held   together,
     when I see bypass

          hold my wrist over
          my heart just to feel
          the beating
inside me

On Innocence
At Quality Waters, NM

I am too young
to handle bone & knife.

Just out of morning
dark glints a rainbow

trout, her life full
as her stomach, her

fins flap like wings,
breaking water, to catch

the last blue of night's
end. Dad squats.

A crowning shimmer
from her exquisite belly,

Here's where you cut—

as he tightens his fist
around her body. Now

gut open, he pulls her
spine, her entrails

caught in current
downstream. Flyaways

bend like grasses
in breeze. My eyes drift

off before watering over—
my blade tip cold

as the deep deep—
down here it's easy

to mistake your hand
for someone else's

sternum or set of ribs. I
drive a stake in the riverbank:

she's chained through,
gills still moving

When It Was Time

I

It was the Time of Few Photos,
in a day when there were more

of us. Really, only a handful
of copies with our faces exist

from that time. From the photo
you could tell it was Easter:

time of reckoning our eggs,
every glittered zigzag glinting

to the age when gods began
to be, my little fingers grip

shells soon to round back
over themselves—or to chip,

already hand-stitched roses
bud on my cardigan: earth

pleats, our faces loose
with dust, hair powdered light,

her eyes giving way to a trail
soon traveled—

II

Already it's morning, dad
sits, brushing his finger

up and down the soles
of our feet, *It's time.*

We begin running
in moon-dark cold.

III

Already my half smile says
even then I'd never allow—

even in its smallest bloom
to make its way into my eyes,

as though I knew in a month's
time—she'd hie to the world

we once loved together
        before me,
land of fountains: where cascades
my joy as exceeding does my grief.

Scaling the Black
At Navajo Dam

A shutter of short strokes all along the body—my father taught me how to scale a fish: with knife's dull edge, from tail to head, at an angle set to barely puncture, until it's blurred to blackness, until each freckle fades into itself: *O wei o na o wei o naa. O wei o na o wei o na'o a'o. O wei o nei o naa o wei o naa.* This evening, a flicker reflect from moon on lake stirs me through current: in times like fresh fish skin. All I know is—*O wei yana, ya weia naa o, wei ya na ahaa, ya wei o nahoho. Ya wei o nei o na, o wei o na.*

The moon has never shone so ugly, and all this wanting smears lake into fish. It piques me to reel in my line. I refuse to dip even the tips of my fingers in this dam, as unclouded as it may seem. When I go to wrap myself in my skirt, huddling on the tongue of a tailgate, I realize even the moon bears wrinkles. In her ridges, loneliness waxes clear as a sucker, even in its thinnest arc. In those final flickers, fire waves me over to cross the lake—I wanted to be at the side of a lollipop, coupled as plain as sugar and water. What beauty comes from her haze? What sweetness wears my hands brittle? The last time I took water, my palms cupped. The last time I tied a knot, I lost my fly and line and hook.

I graze my palms on boulders that shed sand when touched, looking to dodge headlights and fishermen, a cool place to squat unnoticed. Meanwhile my live bait, a grasshopper, makes its way out of my net, and a ways off couples cast their lines into the shallows. With every throw of their arms, they blacken into the sky. And my friends at the shoreline—*I don't even know them.* Nor their dark figures shuffling in the moon's reflection from lake. As I finger through my fly case, the wings remain still. I nudge them to wiggle, wishing the man hadn't come to where I'm casting, where I had hoped a fish would part his lips for my fly.

Until the moon forges me the radiance of her hands, and for all my wanting, I scale cliffs only to reach blacktop.

It's Hard to Write a Love Poem When

always my face skin itches, first along jawbone
women are kneeling creek side to dye ribbon
back muscles ache from wearing velveteen, deep rose
I spend so much time in the gray room, where red flows
women seep by the hundreds back into tree bones

the time has come for my headshot to be shown
for my sister's art installation, so many eyes once shone
so much lint accumulates, quietly I peel off to doze
always my face bone

the love of my life scrubs his scalp among glacier stones
in minutes I have to start my truck to leave, having grown
away go the geese, leaving their white speckled woes
my raspberry jam didn't set again, so now a syrup flows
they say, set her free from tree to sky; like a star she rose
always my face bone—

Candy Dish Sonnet

Already the heart-shaped dish on my end table
lies combed bare: long strips dug out
(   )—a cleaning out
(   ) a scratch in grain, table

scraps lain out so comely, meaning to love
or hold cacao & almonds—those striae
of protein. A deep cut, I tell the butcher,
I'll take the heart as soon as you can give it,

a gift to the first child I come across. Crows
in trees lean in with every crumple the butcher
paper makes in my hand—soon the branches
will be as naked as bone china, and we, like

the skeletal sky, reach out for any sweet filling

Into Rain

when it's too much   to press play
    or to embrace
me again atop the stairs, an upward

pushing away of my skirt, maybe
we should try out our lungs again—

the clouds have come,
    but there's nothing yet

    I would've snapped
your pearl buttons shut
    over and over, just to hear

us click and to feel
the smooth shells down your—

    I would've scooped
water   from the barrel
to your lips   every fifteen minutes
you came   around, had you asked

    instead, you hold a plastic
gallon jug between your knees,
before peeling   the plastic from its neck

saliva is only clean if it comes
straight from the source, you say

    when thunder leaves us
to breathe   in rainfall, left to seep
out our sides—

just when I am no longer   afraid to spill
over and take any ledge or mouth, you gamble
on a side creek
                just when I come

    to drip—

you take Valerian blossom then leave
right as we begin to slide

Of Ribbon

Come tying, the day
we dig arrowheads

from the bottom of a tub,
to wrap twine about the necks

of obsidian. We come around
the rotary, like bark braided

around my neck. It's night now
and I return to the mountain

between my feet, up my legs,
into my body. Nearly

all alone in river
and still, like a single

ripple, left wanting
honeysuckle mornings.

I've felt grass sway inside me
like strands of ribbon

along his ribs. I've seen
him weave his way

into manhood. I know
the shapes his palms make,

ankles and teeth. They slide
then lock into me like rope

burn, fused to each petal
or wing or ripple.

The Warbler
On learning to say

It's mostly soft nothings: when the water cup   is just beyond my reach.
   I'll stand down here, where
      it's safe, where the warble begins to trail   and imitate wrens, how
         they vary their throats: white   into calf love, like dust   storms
      pulled out of the chest
a slow swell of the ear   and creek bed, I kneel on red sand   hand cup
   until entrails just stop—
      Then dissonance altogether like a hard landing into a canyon   nest or
      the splat of white
and deep-green matter   against the bottom of a canyon   this is what
   I was afraid of
         wall, like adjusting frequencies—

      Thank you, Serenity, for running   to the driveway's end   to trill
   the faintest
of tunes, a baby wren   these days it's difficult   for me to switch off
   the radio, the only place
      I'm comfortable in   is silence, is when I sing   to open   land,
   you   helped me by saying
I couldn't love anywhere,   even though it was pretty   for a time; it
   could never   fully echo,
      and that's why   I could only warble, click   my tongue: a
      falling   that didn't lick anything

the phrase had already gone   stale with me. I'd rather   everyone else go

    sour   instead of them

        knowing how I truly—

        thanks to a young girl's easy declaration: it's expanse   of sky

    here, a clearing

        of blue, replete with thought   the canyon wrens, see

    them   unravel their throats

I'll straighten everything to whistle: it does matter, angles cut

    into a greater cascade

    in the splat, it's not: *You I love.*

        It's the song's whole ending

        whole bottom lip—how it's come to quiver.

Night Portrait with Cannon Fire

Oceti Sakowin Camp

there's no fire, not tonight

  clouds bright up for one portrait

we came to tend to—here

    tap boom, boom in chest

from a tent, looking skyward:

  There! There! No, there!

a bedroll offers little comfort,

  at every spark, flash, & lulu—

when battle reaches down from sky

  to throat—earlier today dogs were unleashed—

to shoulder wind this strong

    the wrestle: dark sky seeps into white

then black, silver—*Smile, they say*

    until gum and fang expose themselves

some say they hear a hymn being written

       saliva and song in cannon fire, the fire

works shine up pupil and all—all

       beauty-like and then fall—

face with all its bloomed muscles

       every bone, tooth & blemish

then wilt at clap and circumstance

Pollenback

at the stoplight
my son whispers

Bees, bees
over lavender

stems, lean
into sand waves

they vocal or
dance fly

at the petal
lip, brush against

any fertile up-
standing, sway

with sundown
clouds—

earlier today
we spread ash

across our faces
arms & legs

at the tree line
with smoke

then the light
changes—

Look, son
it's time

for sky, earth-
side to sleep

for flowers
to lie still

atop the cold
atop the cold

Please don't
go, lift

arms, drag
tongue paper

sheets of pollen
grain, these days

bursts of prayer
of falling rays

now, wing flap
for bursts of air

I don't even look
to his forewings

I mean, I
no longer

see his eyes,
just his back

turning away
to churn in pollen—

Portrait of the Gray Room
To 鄭福成

There's nothing I can do; leaves
have gone wilted & pages dust-

covered from years of howling. Desk
wood written through, though on nights

like this I almost believe—but knots
interrupt striae. How can I fly

when Earth carries me this way?
Decades later, I still lament gray

walls and all the light they graze
from me while I sleep. The one

I love an ocean away, years away,
has forgotten bamboo we planted:

I cup these children in a tub of gray
water. We've washed ourselves

into tin again, with only our hands
like a vase on the end table—

Sliding the lamp closer to white,
closer I am to the page—this is grace

in its finest ink. I'm old enough now
to write a love poem, to request

an absentee ballot—mark it up because
the ones I have are near done fading;

the once vibrant moon of Chang Er
and her rabbit, yolk-filled lunar

cakes and gold characters on red
envelopes expressions of every—

We've been pealing as of late. Inside
me, right here—red or black ink,

tin white page of it all: a glass bowl
in dishwater or clean sheets.

Cold & cotton shipping out
of my hands, from my fingers

water: a gush of contrition
face & knee prone to the ground.

This is how I've been meaning to love you—
far inside our home, the walls wait with me

in this light, in this dish, in the fabric:
every shard and stitch absent of you.

)(

Lacing

He seemed nothing more than plastic, opaque
without any emotion wearing down his tongue,
like rain off the leaf of a boy's flower, or muscle ache.
It began like that; he didn't care for me, so young.

We both had pollen falling from our backs.
He said he'd never remember me that way,
when the sky breaks from the throwing of our jacks,
and cracks like veins of a leaf: mid-air, mid-May.

There I was, all spread out for the taking,
waiting to be collected by calloused fists—
We came and went, as if we were lace for the breaking,
our lives rounding out like arcs of our wrists.

We were taught to approach each other the way
we approach land and sky, kneeling together on that day.

I

Dear mother, I pointed my lips like him,
same direction and same tilt of the head:
he loved the ones who confused words said
in bed near window panes, lighting stems
of candles. They'd overheat as if at the gym
and when the flicker eased into a dead
poof, they'd whirl off like smoke, led
enough to get them on their way—a hymn

quivers through me roadside—Dear sir,
this is how my father taught me to leave
water at my mother's graveside. At her wake
her skin laid whist, just like our eyes were
the first time we met. Though I tried to heave,
she seemed nothing more than plastic, opaque.

II

These days I've taken to agreeing with everyone,
I agreed my cousin shouldn't have worn
orange to her father's wedding. I'd rather see it shorn
off her body as if she were a wooly one
of my sheep. I agreed we should have left everyone
waiting in hunger, just to let them ache some—mourn
the sliced neck and belly of a recently worn
lamb. It was its time anyway, I agreed. Everyone

knows what it's like to be sheared, the stubble
that follows the shine. We tend to curl
like the peeled rind of an orange: a lung
or two in its first stage of shrivel falls to rubble,
a dry heaving, and that would be me: the girl
without any emotion wearing down her tongue.

III

Tonight I'm going to show him how I got good
at petitioning for rain, how I came to handle
drowning, and how I came to turn away from candle
light because the flicker simply overwhelmed me. Could
I, in his absence, pass my hands over limbs of wood—
Tonight, though we're walking in years between us, a candle
brings us a cloud closer to a deeper hue, and we can handle
any breeze that turns us inside out. I leave on my hood,
afraid I'll forget I even changed. Forget his whorl.
If he were rain, I'd quit him before he even fell.
I was taught not to run when it finally came, but to take
it all in; I couldn't. It's the way my hands and face whirl
off like utterance in the wind, and my drowning quells
like rain off the leaf of a boy's flower, or muscle ache.

IV

It began: he wouldn't loll with me on the river,
just lie belly down, swivel his body, facing the bank.
I gripped his ankles, when he asked, as his tube sank.
Water has gone chocolate; give indulgence to the giver,
a ribbon. As a child I'd clamber here just to quiver:
descend a fallen cottonwood in marsh to reach the rank
of my solace—there ebbs my shadow in ripples, all dank
and caught up in someone else's mirage: it's begun to shiver.
How long can clouds keep this up?
All thunder and no lightning. Black stirs above us,
neither of us fall in or over or out. All along, I sung
the river to bend, rapids to rise, for him to cup
his torso toward me, just a swerve even, without a fuss—
It began like that; he didn't care for me, so young.

V

We swerve like honeybees, round the mouth
    of a frosted spigot, as if we have no real lives
        to tend to, no real roles in our own stories: hives
    gone gray too soon. This is the time of mouths:
ducts arc into throat. Is this how we really live?
    We drink winter honey, as if lacking couth
        then go back to autumn to mourn the wives
    who fell in the rain, against a blade, now routh
with streaks of—that time we rushed like rain to meet
    along ridges of the Chuskas. Our first flight,
        it's how we came to burst forth from wax.
    The moon hollowed into a hook, hung at our feet,
and in its light from lake to temple, that last night,
    we both had pollen falling from our backs.

VI

We never spoke of fuse or salts before
the day we spent along windows, spooning gray

squash inside us. We were the kind a ways
off from our eyes. And while sunlight wore

us thin, we saw we were not as we were before
masses of pieced faces no longer kept at bay.

I've felt temples with stained leaves; it's like they lay
dancing in still motion until wind caught then tore

through them in a breath's chime. In fog, I won't raise
my eyes to his, won't touch the glass inside me (feel

it long enough to remember my own hands, the way
they once pressed fragile surfaces). Such was I razed,

though I had forgotten every shard beneath my heels—
He said he'd never remember me that way.

VII

Sometimes I kneel down to play a game
from my childhood. Only then can I feel
grains of gravel, each pebble digs in so real.
Sometimes I act as though I am the same,
a young girl, rope in hand, at the tetherball game:
I blare out rule after rule and feel them peal
within me, as though I'm chanting to be healed
from some minor infraction. It's lame,
to say the least, to be kneeling alone
with socks full of holes—so he came to play.
From the lining of his vest, he took out jacks
and a small rubber ball. *You're not here alone*,
he said before throwing his with mine. Let's play
until the sky breaks from the throwing of our jacks.

VIII

Believe me; it's more than breath or shine
that's kept us from falling. T'was a glance
from a dark time paused for a slow dance.

I'm not sure when he became benign:
leaf scar. In rhythm, down the vine,
caught by a blossom, thrown in a trance

by its death. Thus is the desert's stance:
lone, kneading into itself. In fine,
that's how I saw him, the way he left

me—crisp as a leaf, we noted scars
and passed to the passings—still, I'll gray
best I can, waft this way & that, bereft—

I happen in like a line of scars:
crack like veins of leaves: mid-air, mid-May.

IX

There I was, all spread out for the taking,
bloomed wings waiting for winter
sleet. It was a long season of drinking whole
creeks and nothing else. We churned desert
into desert. What I'm saying is, neither the desert
rat nor damselfly can bear the nosebleeds: shoal-
laced face bearing down just in time to overwinter.
There I was, all spread out for the taking.

In truth, nobody wants water this thin.
One swallow, and we're off to dig for more within
a hollow womb. This morning we sip water,
discussing the trauma in our blood: saltwater—
there it rests, in droplets, on my breast skin,
Oh, I say. *My tears*, rubbing them deep within.

X

I lie still as a hanger
beneath a crib, forgotten lint
mountain backs ridging
all about me, so tonight, from my throat

spores unlodge into a hailstorm.
Here the scarf is a body giving way
to wind—on a ledge—our legs
drape like burlap from the tailgate,

and in this breeze, I still hang
my hair and skin the same. *Hang
in there*, I say. *I'm giving up on you.*
Then reach over to touch his back.
This morning it's just the lint and me
waiting to be collected by calloused fists.

XI

At church I sat salvaged: I said to send me
away wearing nothing but satin and lace.
We both felt secondhand. It was knee-
length, and it wore me cheap. I couldn't embrace
the old woman who once wore it, couldn't see
my wrists even. And my neck, it was braced
up all in lace. The woman next to me says,
How beautiful. I say, *This beautiful,* then split
a hair down the middle. I lied, *I made it myself,*
then stood up to fade through painstaking
humiliation. As a child, a girl, I saw through myself
to age 82. It was then when I first noticed the aching
of my hands, how they were soon to set themselves
away—they came and went, as if they were lace for the breaking.

XII

The lace hem of my skirt has become worn.
Or maybe it's always been this way: like wind,
we never felt the cracks of morn

that summer. I told him I'd turn them, wind
them even, if he wanted me to, until he'd think
I was making music—sometimes when I bind

them, they can be tuned beautiful still. Just a wink,
and I'll come wearing mountains over my shoulders,
come bearing lakes about my legs. Then in a blink

we'll tune ourselves to a field of lace, our shoulder
blades thrusting into the white, and our wrists—
they'll finish going round, ready to shoulder

the day we yellow together into old lace, old wrists.
Our lives rounded out like arcs of our wrists.

XIII

I was reciting Lord Alfred Tennyson on my back,
in a canoe, floating the holiest way I knew—
so close to ghost, and went pale for a moment
before finding myself wandering among high pines.

I didn't expect to emerge in white already
with my heart in his hand, just as normal
as a shell rests on my chest. Didn't expect
to hand it over so early on, at the boundary

of our properties in a dream: in the grasses
where he ended and I began. *I'm feeling very still*
now that we've crossed over into the pale,
where we are soon to thread, soon to embellish,

then loop back into each other: braided the way
we were taught to approach each other—the same way.

XIV

From the mountainside we appear
to wear each other deep into the road.
We appear in the braids of slowed
water at our knees, as though prepared

for a ritual among the falls. It breaks
all around us—lace in its final wear.
We nearly swallow ourselves, bare
every blue we have to give, until lakes

settle in with the stars. We came to see
stars wiggle, to wander the unknowing
grays & blues until finally, our flowing
bares our wrists: I wade for you, and see,

the stars wade for you—resting on an altar crochet,
we approach land and sky, kneeling together on that day.

Notes

"Sonnet for My Wrist": Italicized text is from Wake Singers' "Human Devil."

"Round Our Wrists": Italicized text is adapted from Denis Johnson's "The Boarding."

"Lacing": Italicized text in section XIII is from David Bowie's "Space Oddity."

Acknowledgments

Sending immense gratitude to the editors of journals and anthologies that gave initial homes to the poems found in this collection:

The Arkansas International: "The Warbler"

As/Us Journal: "Lace Sonnet"

Blossom as the Cliffrose: Mormon Legacies and the Beckoning Wild: "Lacing XIV"

Contra Viento: "Lacing II" and "Lacing VIII"

Crazyhorse: "Chafe" and "Sonnet for My Wrist"

Dialogue: A Journal of Mormon Thought: "Candy Dish Sonnet" and "Lacing VII"

Dispatches Journal: "Lacing III" and "Lacing XII"

EPOCH Magazine: "Lacing IV," Lacing V," and "Lacing X"

Hairstreak Butterfly: "Portrait of the Gray Room"

The Hopkins Review: "The Night My Wrist Broke"

House Mountain Review: "Pollenback"

Kenyon Review Online: "Round Our Wrists"

Literary Hub: "Into Rain"

Literature and Belief: "A February Snow"

Mandala Journal: "Scaling the Black"

The Memory of Stone: Meditations on the Canyons of the West: "Hole through the Rock"

New Poets of Nation Nations: "Hole through the Rock"

Orogeny: "Lacing II," "Lacing VIII," "Lacing IX," "Lacing XI," and "Lacing XIII"

Partial Zine: "It's Hard to Write a Love Poem When"

Poem-A-Day: Academy of American Poets: "River Sonnet" (now "River Silt")

Poetics for the More-than-Human World: An Anthology of Poetry and Commentary: "Lacing III" and "Lacing VII"

POETRY: "Lacing IX," "Lacing XI," "Lacing XIII," and "Apricot Lament"

Raleigh Review: "Last Night, Bleeding"

The Rumpus: "Sang Over"

Shenandoah: "Bird Dance" and "Gown Sonnet"

Stonecoast Review: "Out of Star"

Talking River: "Lacing"

Thalia Magazine: "A Blood Letting"

When the Light of the World Was Subdued, Our Songs Came Through: A Norton Anthology of Native Nations Poetry: "Sonnet for My Wrist"

World Literature Today: "Still Life Morrow"

Yellow Medicine Review: "Querido Apu" and "Twist Implied" (now "Of Ribbon"); "On Innocence," "Lacing I," and "Lacing VI"

ZOCALA Public Square: "When It Was Time"

~

With great appreciation to those who invited me to read these poems at their events and institutions, it was wonderful meeting you all, and you've kept my life busy with doing what I love: travel and poetry.

To the University of Wisconsin Press staff, editors, and director, and Eduardo C. Corral, thank you for *seeing* my work and letting it here be seen.

To my writer circle, whose friendships and words continually nourish and inspire me. Please insert you name here: _____, and especially to Landis Grenville: your spirit is in these pages.

To my literary aunties, Jane Hafen, Heid E. Erdrich, Esther Belin, Luci Tapahonso, Laura Tohe, Joy Harjo, Deborah Miranda, Elise Paschen, Denise Low, Kimberly Blaeser, Layli Long Solider, dg nanouk okpik, and the many others.

To Jim Barnes for introducing me to received forms, including the sonnet, and for your and Kandi's friendship.

To Cara Romero, for your brilliant and stirring work.

With great thanks to those of my classmates—too many to name—who offered generous feedback as I've finished up my final revisions of this book as a PhD student at Florida State University, and especially to my professors James Kimbrell, Virgilio Suarez, Barbara Hamby, David Kirby, and Lamar Wilson.

And for the content, thank you to the men who kept my premarriage years interesting: full of wonder, delight, heartbreak, and hope. To the ones I've looked on from afar with much ardor, thank you for keeping me preserved. To the ones whose wrists I never took or dropped, I *am* sorry, but know you have enriched my life. I wish you every joy.

To my bff and soul sister April Sunshine Sanchez, who, for decades, has been a light and support to me and my family, who has taken countless calls, made dozens of trips and cross-country drives with me, and whose heart knows and cares about every story here—faleminderit.

To my dad, who raised me and my siblings as a single father; I could not have done it without your love: teachings, support, and encouragement all my life.

Always, love to my husband, who is not present in these poems because we had not yet met; you are my heart, my life, and I walk with you through eternity.

And last, but most certainly not least, to my Heavenly Father, who guides me and lights my mind and words, thank you. For your unfailing love, for the blessings you constantly and continually send, ahéhee'.

TACEY M. ATSITTY, Diné (Navajo), is Tsénahabiłnii (Sleep Rock People) and born for Ta'neeszahnii (Tangle People). The recipient of numerous prizes and fellowships, Atsitty is an inaugural Indigenous Nations Poets fellow and holds degrees from Brigham Young University and the Institute of American Indian Arts as well as an MFA from Cornell University. The author of *Rain Scald* (University of New Mexico Press), Atsitty has also published work in *POETRY*, *EPOCH*, *Kenyon Review Online*, *Poem-A-Day: Academy of American Poets*, *The Hopkins Review*, *Shenandoah*, *High Country News*, *Hairstreak Butterfly Review*, *Literature and Belief*, *Leavings*, and other publications. She is the director of the Navajo Film Festival, a member of the Advisory Board for BYU's Charles Redd Center for Western Studies, and a board member for Lightscatter Press. Atsitty is a PhD candidate in creative writing at Florida State University in Tallahassee, where she lives with her husband.

WISCONSIN POETRY SERIES

Sean Bishop and Jesse Lee Kercheval, *series editors*
Ronald Wallace, *founding series editor*

(B) = Winner of the Brittingham Prize in Poetry
(FP) = Winner of the Felix Pollak Prize in Poetry
(4L) = Winner of the Four Lakes Prize in Poetry
(T) = Winner of the Wisconsin Prize for Poetry in Translation